LIONEL BART'S

OLIVER!

Book, Music
and Lyrics
by Lionel Bart

—— *Winner of:* ——

6 ACADEMY AWARDS
including
BEST PICTURE *and* BEST DIRECTOR (1968)
3 TONY AWARDS (1963)
3 IVOR NOVELLO AWARDS (1960)
1 OLIVIER AWARD (1994)

ISBN 978-0-634-02393-4

TRO│ESSEX
MUSIC GROUP

EXCLUSIVELY DISTRIBUTED BY

HAL•LEONARD®

Visit Hal Leonard Online at
www.halleonard.com

Contact us:
Hal Leonard
7777 West Bluemound Road
Milwaukee, WI 53213
Email: info@halleonard.com

In Europe, contact:
Hal Leonard Europe Limited
42 Wigmore Street
Marylebone, London, W1U 2RN
Email: info@halleonardeurope.com

In Australia, contact:
Hal Leonard Australia Pty. Ltd.
4 Lentara Court
Cheltenham, Victoria, 3192 Australia
Email: info@halleonard.com.au

❧ BACKGROUND ❧

The Charles Dickens novel *Oliver Twist* at this writing has been made into three major dramatic film versions, the latest directed by Roman Polanski. The 1922 silent film directed by Frank Lloyd starred Lon Chaney as Fagin with Jackie Coogan as Oliver. The 1948 David Lean film starred Alec Guinness as Fagin and Anthony Newley played the Artful Dodger. The Lionel Bart musical stage version *Oliver!* has also seen the mark of different directors and actors as well, and even the music has had variations.

The original London production, directed by Peter Coe was for the most part transferred to Broadway where it became the longest running British musical in Broadway history until it was toppled by *Cats* in the 80s. Even the female lead Nancy played by Georgia Brown was the same. The part of Fagin played by Ron Moody in London changed to Clive Revill, but in the short run Broadway revival some 20 years later, the part was again played by Moody. Barry Humphries, later known as Dame Edna, followed the show to Broadway as Mr. Sowerberry, the undertaker. He later would play the role of Fagin at the Piccadilly Theatre in London. In 1997 he also played Fagin for a month in the Cameron Mackintosh production, the longest running show in the history of the London Palladium. The 1997 Cameron Mackintosh revival opened with Jonathan Pryce as Fagin. The role of Fagin was also played by Jim Dale, Russ Abbot and Robert Lindsay. The 1984 Broadway revival didn't fare so well. Even with Ron Moody as Fagin and Patti LuPone as Nancy, the production closed after 17 performances.

Besides Lionel Bart's book, music and lyrics, the original 1960 production's greatest asset was Sean Kenny's set. *Oliver!* looked like no previous musical. An ever-revolving wood and steel construction of staircases, platforms and bridges instantly created new locations with cinematic fluidity. The plot was propelled by the design. When Cameron Mackintosh's 1994 London revival was taking shape, he realized he had to put together a completely new *Oliver!* Sam Mendes, the new director, suggested Anthony Ward for design and Matthew Bourne for choreography. Lionel Bart added new lyrics and music which was orchestrated by Bill Brohn.

Mark Lester as Oliver in the 1968 Motion Picture.

The score to the multi Academy Award winning 1968 *Oliver!* was by John Green, and included an extra verse to "Where Is Love?" The heart-rending ballad "As Long As He Needs Me" had earlier made the Billboard popular music charts in 1963 with a modified lyric sung by Sammy Davis, Jr.. *Oliver!* is unquestionably a classic, a perennial with school and amateur groups, and its individual songs are among the most recorded and performed.

The Original 1963 Broadway Cast, with Clive Revill (Fagin), Danny Sewell (Bill Sikes), and Georgia Brown (Nancy). Photo courtesy of Photofest.

Show art from 1994 West End Revival.

OLIVER!

CONTENTS

Fagin (Clive Revill), The Artful Dodger (David Jones) and the boys from the 1963 Broadway Production. Photo courtesy of Photofest.

❧ SYNOPSIS ❧

Act One

The curtain opens on the grim hall of a 19th century London workhouse with a bare dining table where Oliver Twist and the orphan boys who toil there will receive their daily ration of gruel. They file to the table and sing **Food, Glorious Food**. After they have wolfed down their meager fare, Oliver politely asks for more. Mr. Bumble, a minor parish official, and Widow Corney, workhouse supervisor, are appalled. They and the boys sing the derisive **Oliver!**.

In Corney's room, she and Mr. Bumble take a moment out for some gin-laced tea and flirtation (**I Shall Scream**) before effecting Oliver's punishment. Bumble then leads Oliver off singing the haunting **Boy for Sale.** Walking through the streets of London, they arrive at the establishment of undertaker Mr. Sowerberry, who accepts Oliver because his melancholy face suggests he might make a suitable "coffin follower." Sowerberry, his wife and Mr. Bumble sing **That's Your Funeral**. Left alone to sleep among the coffins, Oliver expresses the understandable emotions of a frightened, unloved child (**Where Is Love?**).

He runs away the next morning and is picked up by The Artful Dodger who cheers him up with **Consider Yourself.** He leads Oliver through the streets to the Thieves' Kitchen where he is welcomed by Fagin who gives him instructions on what is to be Oliver's new vocation: **Pick a Pocket or Two**. Oliver meets the others in Fagin's circle, Bet, and the beautiful Nancy, who is in love with the thug Bill Sikes. The two of them, accompanied by the boys and Fagin, celebrate their way of life in **It's a Fine Life** and then all mock polite society by singing **I'd Do Anything**.

The next morning Fagin sends Oliver and the boys off on a pick-pocketing expedition with a festive send-off, **Be Back Soon**. But things go awry. Well-to-do Mr. Brownlow is the Dodger's victim but innocent newcomer Oliver is blamed and dragged off by the police as the curtain falls.

"Consider Yourself": Jack Wild as The Artful Dodger and Mark Lester as Oliver Twist from the 1968 Motion Picture.

"Please, sir, I want some more." Mark Lester from the 1968 Motion Picture.

"I'd Do Anything": Bet (Sheila White), Oliver (Mark Lester), Nancy (Shani Wallis) and cast from the 1968 Motion Picture.

"Who Will Buy"
from the 1968 Motion Picture.

Act Two

At the Three Cripples, an underworld tavern, Nancy sings a music-hall number, **Oom-Pah-Pah**. Bill Sikes then silences the crowd with his menacing entrance (**My Name**). Meanwhile, Oliver's innocence has been established and he has been taken into the home of the kindly Mr. Brownlow. Bill is concerned that Oliver will reveal the gang's doings and forces Nancy to get Oliver back. Reluctantly she admits that her love for Bill means she will do what he wants (**As Long as He Needs Me**).

In his new-found luxurious home, Oliver looks out his bedroom window, and accompanied by the cries of street vendors, wishes that his happiness will last (**Who Will Buy?**). Later he is sent on an errand, is seized by Nancy and Bill and taken back to Fagin's. A violent argument over the treatment of Oliver leaves Fagin considering the possibility of going straight (**Reviewing the Situation**).

Back at the workhouse, the now unhappily married Bumble and Corney discover that Oliver is from a wealthy family and decide they must retrieve him (**Oliver! Reprise**). Bumble's visit and report to Brownlow confirms that Oliver is the illegitimate child of Brownlow's deceased daughter. Nancy arrives, regretting her part in Oliver's capture, and promises to return him at night on the London Bridge. (**As Long as He Needs Me Reprise**).

Nancy keeps her word but unfortunately Bill follows her. He murders Nancy and takes the boy. After a chase he is shot dead. Oliver is restored to his grandfather. Fagin, whose den has been raided, again considers turning over a new leaf (**Reviewing the Situation Reprise**). The entire cast returns for a final medley of **Food, Glorious Food, Consider Yourself,** and **I'd Do Anything**.

"As Long As He Needs Me":
Shani Wallis from the 1968 Motion Picture.

❦ Lionel Bart (1930-1999) ❦

Born in London to Galician Jews, Bart changed his last name Begleiter to Bart after St. Bartholomew's Hospital (Bart's). His musical talent was recognized at a young age but he was undisciplined, and attempts to teach him the violin were unsuccessful. He never learned to read or write musical notation, but this didn't stop him from becoming a highly significant personality in the development of British rock and pop music.

Cited by none other than Andrew Lloyd Webber as the father of the modern British musical, Lionel Bart was the composer, book writer and lyricist of *Oliver!*, freely adapted from the Charles Dickens novel *Oliver Twist*. Bart was central to the rekindling of musicals in the UK at a time when American productions dominated the West End stage.

Oliver! followed the 1959 successes of *Lock Up Your Daughters*, for which Bart wrote the lyrics to Laurie Johnson's music. Bart's first musical, *Fings Ain't Wot They Used T'Be*, had a two year run in London. At his peak he was also among Britain's top songwriters, penning hits for the likes of Shirley Bassey, Anthony Newley, Tommy Steele ("Rock with the Cavemen," top 20 in 1957) and Cliff Richard ("Living Doll," #1 in 1959). In 1957 he won three Ivor Novello Awards, four more in 1958 and two in 1960. He also wrote the famous James Bond theme, "From Russia With Love" (1964).

Then came two ambitious, operatic and admired musicals, *Blitz!* (1962), a spectacular, moving evocation of wartime London, and *Maggie May* (1964), a Jesus parable set among the dockworkers of contemporary Liverpool. Both featured Sean Kenny designs. But in 1965 Bart met with disaster when he attempted his take on Sherwood Forest and Robin Hood in *Twang!!* This and the Broadway one-nighter *La Strada* began a decline in his theatre career, which lasted for much of the 1970s and 80s.

In 1989 he appeared in a building society television commercial singing "Happy Endings" to a group of children. The song caught on and was issued as a single. The 1990s saw renewed success for his musicals. *Maggie May* and *Blitz!* were revived in the West End and his profile rose through Sir Cameron Mackintosh's 1994 production of *Oliver!* at the Palladium. At the time of his death in 1999 he was working on a revival of the 1969 musical *La Strada*.

Lionel Bart
Photo courtesy of Photofest.

❧ SHOW FACTS ❧

1960 ORIGINAL LONDON PRODUCTION
Producer: Donald Albery for Donmar Productions Ltd.
Director: Peter Coe
Musical Director: Marcus Dods
Set Designer: Sean Kenny
Principal Cast: Ron Moody (Fagin), Georgia Brown (Nancy), Keith Hamshere (Oliver), Paul Whitsun-Jones (Mr. Bumble), Hope Jackman (Widow Corney), Danny Sewell (Bill Sikes), Martin Horsey (Artful Dodger), Barry Humphries (Mr. Sowerberry), Sonia Frasier (Mrs. Sowerberry), Diane Gray (Bet), Madeleine Newbury (Mrs. Bedwin), George Bishop (Mr. Brownlow)
London run: New Theatre, June 30, 1960; 2,618 p.
Awards: Ivor Novello Awards 1960: Outstanding Score of a Stage Play, Film, TV Program or Radio Production (Oliver!); Best Selling and Most Performed Song, Outstanding Song (As Long as He Needs Me)
Cast Recording: Decca Broadway CD

1963 ORIGINAL BROADWAY PRODUCTION
Producers: David Merrick & Donald Albery
Director: Peter Coe
Musical Director: Donald Pippin
Set Designer: Sean Kenny
Principal Cast: Clive Revill (Fagin), Georgia Brown (Nancy), Bruce Prochnik (Oliver), Willoughby Goddard (Mr. Bumble), Hope Jackman (Widow Corney), Danny Sewell (Bill Sikes), David Jones (Artful Dodger), Barry Humphries (Mr. Sowerberry), Helena Carroll (Mrs. Sowerberry), Alice Playten (Bet), Dortha Duckworth (Mrs. Bedwin), Geoffrey Lumb (Mr. Brownlow)
New York run: Imperial Theatre, January 6, 1963; 774 p.
Awards: 3 Tony Awards: Best composer and lyricist, best conductor and musical director, best scenic design
Cast Recording: RCA Victor CD

Stage Performing Rights
These rights are handled
by Tams Witmark.

1994 WEST END REVIVAL
Producer: Cameron Mackintosh
Director: Sam Mendes
Musical Director: Martin Koch
Musical Staging: Matthew Bourne
Set Designer: Anthony Ward
Principal Cast: Jonathan Pryce (Fagin), Sally Dexter (Nancy), Gregory Bradley (Oliver), James Saxon (Mr. Bumble), Jenny Galloway (Widow Corney), Miles Anderson (Bill Sikes), Adam Searles (Artful Dodger), David Delve (Mr. Sowerberry), Mrs. Sowerberry (Julia Deakin), Rosalind James (Bet), Carmel McSharry (Mrs. Bedwin), James Villiers (Mr. Brownlow)
London run: The London Palladium, December 8, 1994; 1,366 p.
Awards: Olivier Award: Best actor in a musical (Robert Lindsay)
Cast Recording: First Night CD

1968 COLUMBIA PICTURES FILM
Screenplay: Vernon Harris
Producer: John Woolf
Director: Carol Reed
Art Direction-Set Decoration: John Box, Terence Marsh, Vernon Dixon, Ken Muggleston
Film score: John Green
Choreographer: Onna White
Cinematographer: Oswald Morris
Principal Cast: Ron Moody (Fagin), Shani Wallis (Nancy), Mark Lester (Oliver), Harry Secombe (Mr. Bumble), Peggy Mount (Widow Corney), Oliver Reed (Bill Sikes), Jack Wild (Artful Dodger), Leonard Rossiter (Mr. Sowerberry), Hylda Baker (Mrs. Sowerberry), Sheila White (Bet), Megs Jenkins (Mrs. Bedwin), Joseph O'Conor (Mr. Brownlow)
Release Date: December 1968; 153 minutes
Awards: 5 Oscars (1969): Best Picture, Director, Art Direction-Set Decoration, Sound, Score of a Musical Picture (Original or Adaptation); 2 Golden Globes (1969): Best Picture-Musical, Actor-Musical (Ron Moody); Golden Prize/Moscow International Film Festival (1969): Best Actor (Ron Moody, tie); Golden Laurel (1970): Musical
Soundtrack Recording: RCA CD
DVD: Columbia/Tristar

Original 1960
London Cast
Recording.

1994 West End
Revival Recording.

OLIVER!
FOOD, GLORIOUS FOOD

Words and Music by
LIONEL BART

OLIVER!
OLIVER!

Words and Music by
LIONEL BART

* The italicized lyrics are from the film.

OLIVER!
I SHALL SCREAM

Words and Music by
LIONEL BART

Widow Corney (spoken): *Mr. Bumble, I shall scream!*

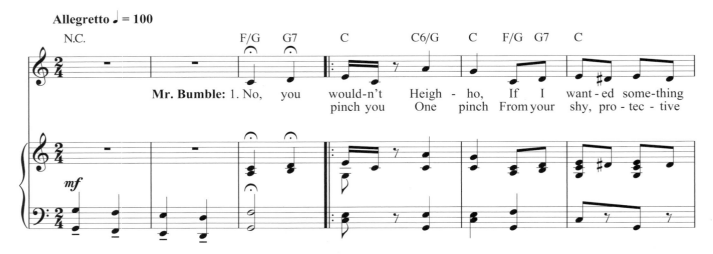

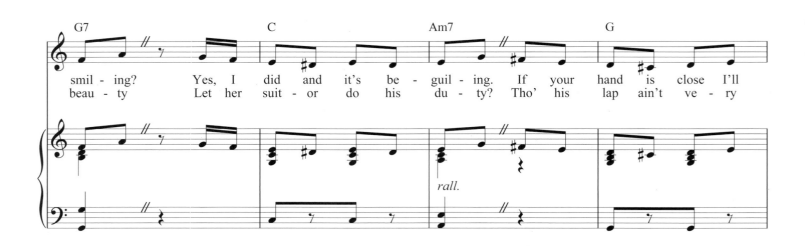

* In the show, Mr. Bumble's voice is muffled by Widow Corney's ample bosom.

OLIVER!
BOY FOR SALE

Words and Music by
LIONEL BART

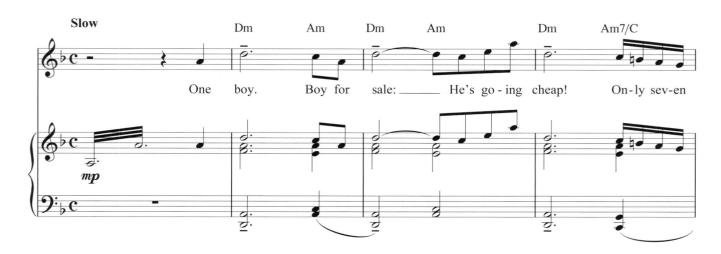

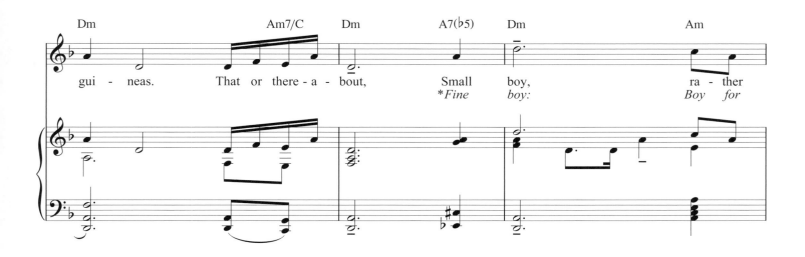

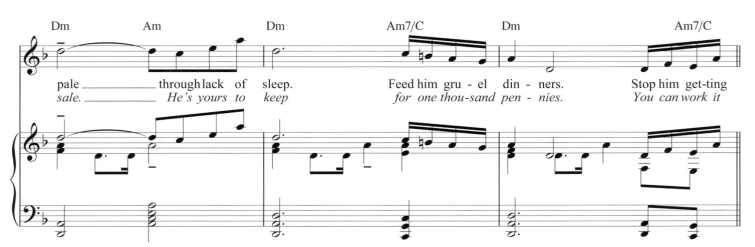

*Italicized lyrics used in film.

THAT'S YOUR FUNERAL

OLIVER!

Words and Music by
LIONEL BART

* Mrs. Sowerberry

WHERE IS LOVE?

Original sheet music from the 1963 Broadway Production.

OLIVER!
WHERE IS LOVE?

Words and Music by
LIONEL BART

* In the film, Oliver sings the italicized lyrics the second time.

OLIVER!
CONSIDER YOURSELF

Words and Music by
LIONEL BART

OLIVER!
PICK A POCKET OR TWO

Words and Music by
LIONEL BART

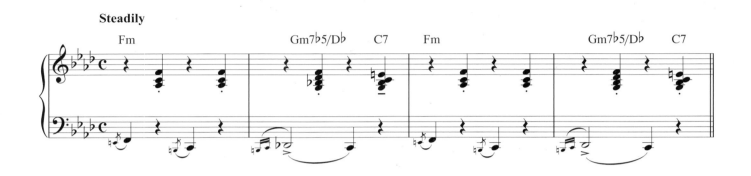

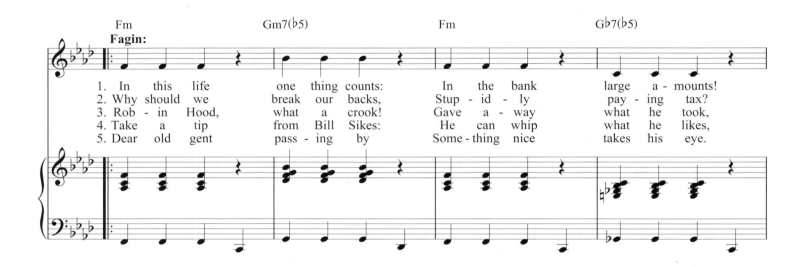

1. In this life one thing counts: In the bank large a - mounts!
2. Why should we break our backs, Stup - id - ly pay - ing tax?
3. Rob - in Hood, what a crook! Gave a - way what he took,
4. Take a tip from Bill Sikes: He can whip what he likes,
5. Dear old gent pass - ing by Some - thing nice takes his eye.

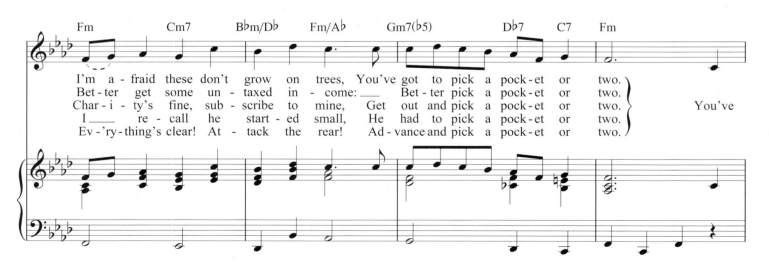

I'm a - fraid these don't grow on trees, You've got to pick a pock - et or two.
Bet - ter get some un - taxed in - come: Bet - ter pick a pock - et or two.
Char - i - ty's fine, sub - scribe to mine, Get out and pick a pock - et or two.
I ___ re - call he start - ed small, He had to pick a pock - et or two.
Ev - 'ry - thing's clear! At - tack the rear! Ad - vance and pick a pock - et or two.
You've

"Pick a Pocket or Two"
Ron Moody as Fagin with the boys from the 1968 Motion Picture.

Clive Revill as Fagin from the 1963 Broadway Production.
Photo courtesy of Photofest.

IT'S A FINE LIFE

OLIVER!

Words and Music by
LIONEL BART

Moderately

1. Small pleas - ures, small pleas - ures, who would de - ny us these?
2. Who cares if straight lac - es sneer at us in the street.
3. No flounc - es, no feath - ers, No frills and fur - bi - loes.

Gin tod - dies, large meas - ures, No skimp - ing if you please!
Fine airs and large fine grac - es Don't have to sin to eat.
All winds and all weath - ers Ain't good for fan - cy clo'es.

OLIVER!
I'D DO ANYTHING

Words and Music by
LIONEL BART

*1st time Dodger, 2nd time Oliver

OLIVER!
I'D DO ANYTHING–REPRISE

Words and Music by
LIONEL BART

OLIVER!
BE BACK SOON

Words and Music by
LIONEL BART

Brightly

1. You can go but be back soon. You can go, but while you're
go, but be back soon. You can go but bring back

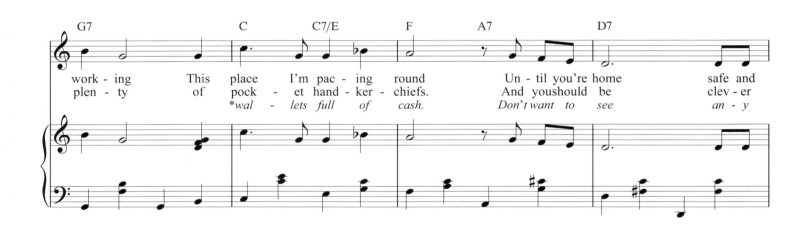

work - ing This place I'm pac - ing round Un - til you're home safe and
plen - ty of pock - et hand - ker - chiefs. And you should be clev - er
*wal - lets full of cash. Don't want to see an - y

sound. Fare thee well, but be back soon. Who can tell where dan - ger's
thieves. Whip it quick and be back soon. There's a six - pence here for
trash. On - ly thick ones now, none

*Additional lyrics used in film.

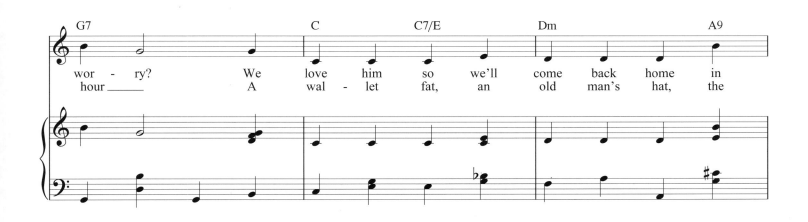

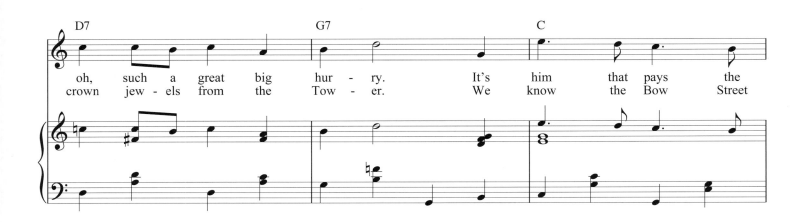

48

* nosey p'licemen (film)

** The film version is as presented here. The stage version states each part separately at first.

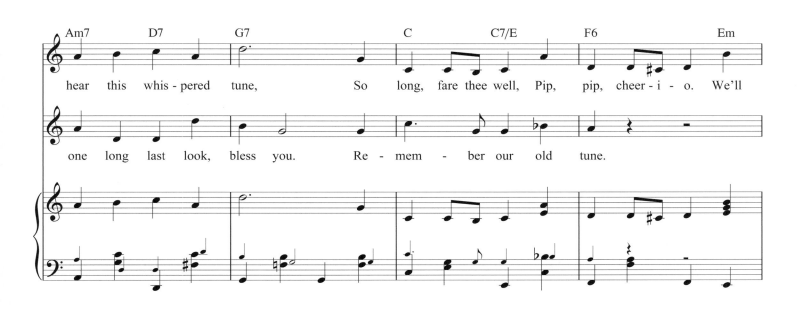

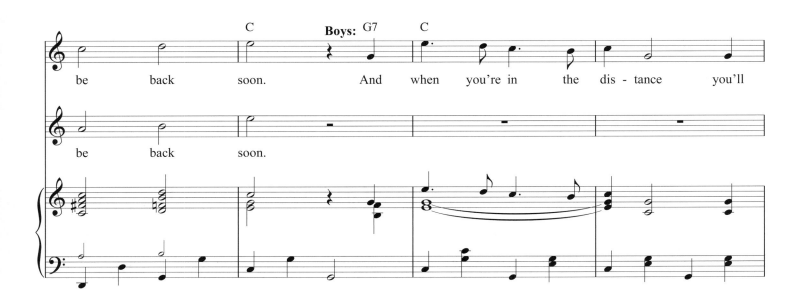

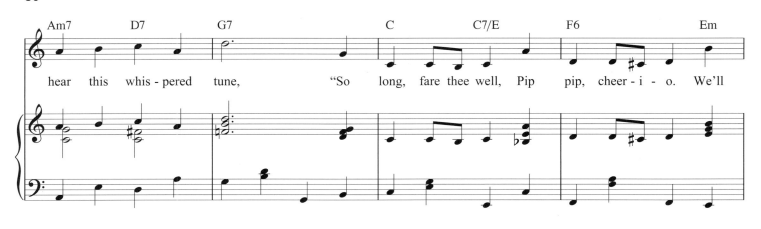

hear this whis-pered tune, "So long, fare thee well, Pip pip, cheer-i-o. We'll

be back soon! **Oliver and Dodger:** So long, fare thee well, Pip

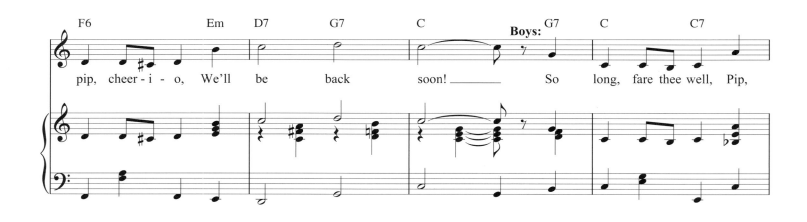

pip, cheer-i-o, We'll be back soon! **Boys:** So long, fare thee well, Pip,

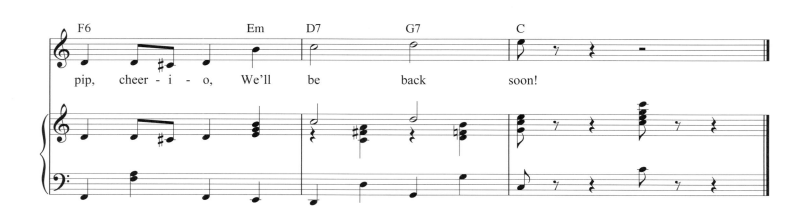

pip, cheer-i-o, We'll be back soon!

OLIVER!
OOM-PAH-PAH

Words and Music by
LIONEL BART

MY NAME

Words and Music by
LIONEL BART

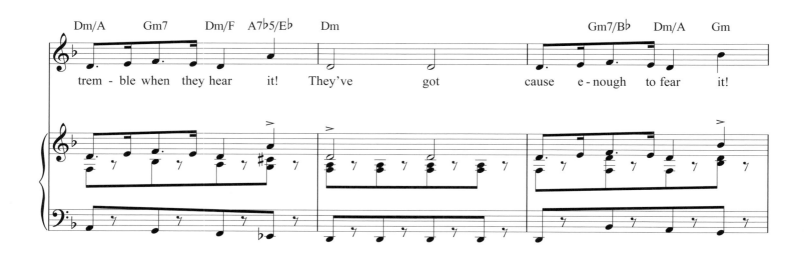

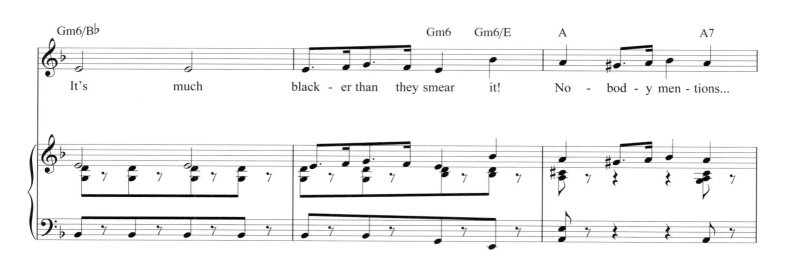

OLIVER!
AS LONG AS HE NEEDS ME

Words and Music by
LIONEL BART

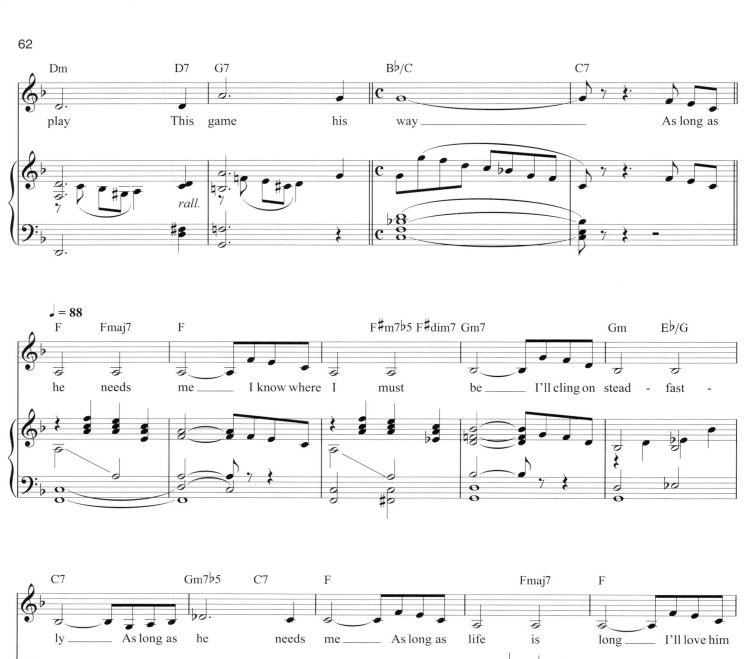

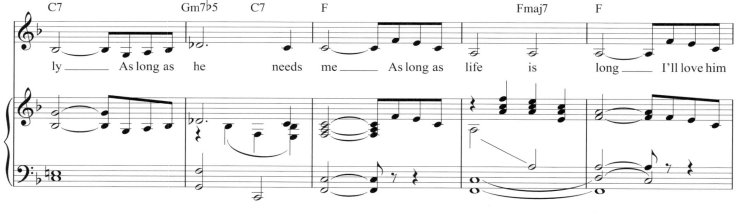

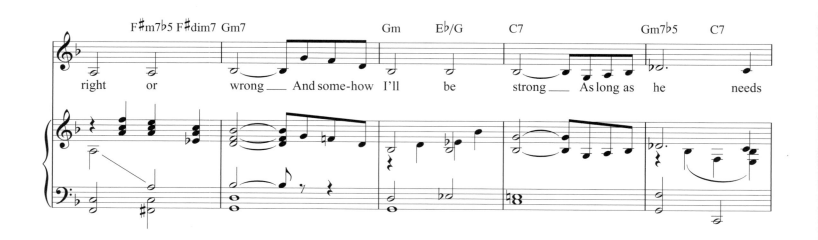

63

Oliver!

WHO WILL BUY?

Words and Music by
LIONEL BART

Me, oh, my, I don't want to lose ___ it, so what am I to

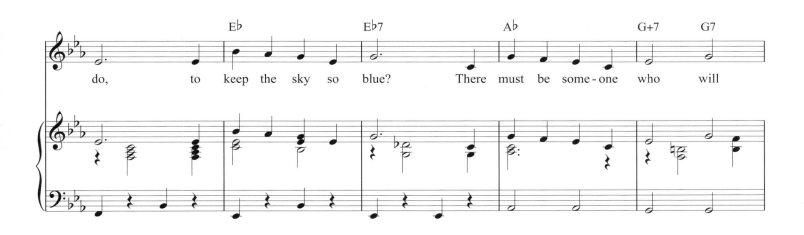

do, to keep the sky so blue? There must be some-one who will

buy. ___ buy. ___

OLIVER!
REVIEWING THE SITUATION

Words and Music by
LIONEL BART

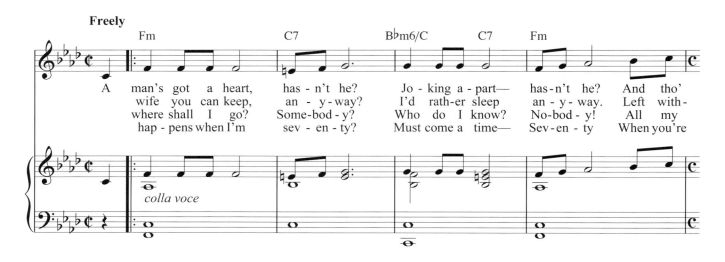

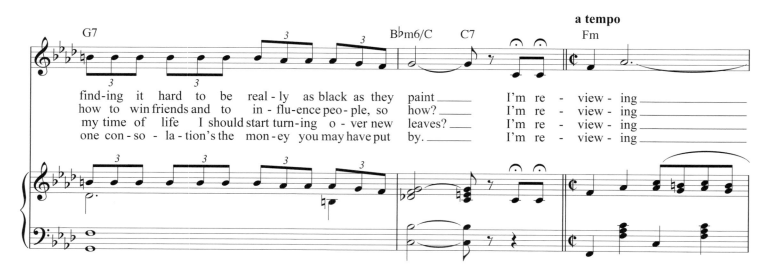

* The italicized lyrics appear in the film as the last verse.